A Green Kid's Guide to
Gardening!

A Green Kid's Guide to
Organic Fertilizers

by Richard Lay
illustrated by Laura Zarrin

magic
wagon

visit us at
www.abdopublishing.com

Printed in the United States of America, North Mankato, MN.
102012
012013
 This book contains at least 10% recycled materials.

Text by Richard Lay
Illustrations by Laura Zarrin
Edited by Stephanie Hedlund and Rochelle Baltzer
Interior layout and design by Renée LaViolette
Cover design by Renée LaViolette

Library of Congress Cataloging-in-Publication Data
Lay, Richard.
  A green kid's guide to organic fertilizers / by Richard Lay ; illustrated by Laura Zarrin.
        p. cm. -- (A green kid's guide to gardening!)
  ISBN 978-1-61641-945-5
1. Organic fertilizers--Juvenile literature. I. Zarrinnaal, Laura Nienhaus. II. Title. III. Series: Lay, Richard. Green kid's guide to gardening!
  S654.L39 2013
  631.8'6--dc23
                        2012023791

Table of Contents

Ice Cream Every Day!

Would you like to eat only ice cream? Some children would say yes. It would taste great and give you energy.

But this would be a problem. You might get sick. It is not a good idea to eat only one type of food. Your body needs different foods to make it healthy and strong.

Gardeners are people who grow plants. "Being green" means learning how to live on Earth without hurting it. A green gardener knows that plants need many different kinds of food. They use organic fertilizers to make healthy soil without hurting Earth.

Do You Have Worms?

Healthy soil has many things in it. It has food and vitamins plants can use. It has dead plants and animals. It has creatures such as bacteria and bugs. But the most important thing healthy soil has is worms.

Good soil has many worms. That is because worms eat organic things in the dirt and then poop. Their poop is called castings. These castings are full of food that plants can use. The castings also make spaces in the soil so that air and water can get into it.

How do you know if your soil has worms? Look at the birds. Some birds, including robins, love to eat worms. If you see robins in your garden, then you have lots of worms. If not, then your soil may not be very healthy.

Feed Your Worms

Worms make healthy soil. But how do you get them? You cannot buy them. If your soil does not have worm food, the worms will leave. There are three foods a green gardener can use to bring in worms.

The first is compost. Compost is a mixture of dirt, dead plants, and small creatures. Compost is the best food for worms. It is also the best food for plants.

The second thing that will draw worms is mulch. When your parents mow your yard, ask them to save the grass they cut. Then put this mulch on the soil in your garden and around the plants. Worms will eat this.

There are other organic mulches. Newspaper and cardboard can be a covering for your garden. Both are made from trees. You could also buy straw from a garden shop or feed store.

The third food a green gardener can use is called green manure. To make green manure, plant winter rye grass in the fall. In the spring turn the soil over. The grass will die in the ground. The dead grass will add lots of food for your worms.

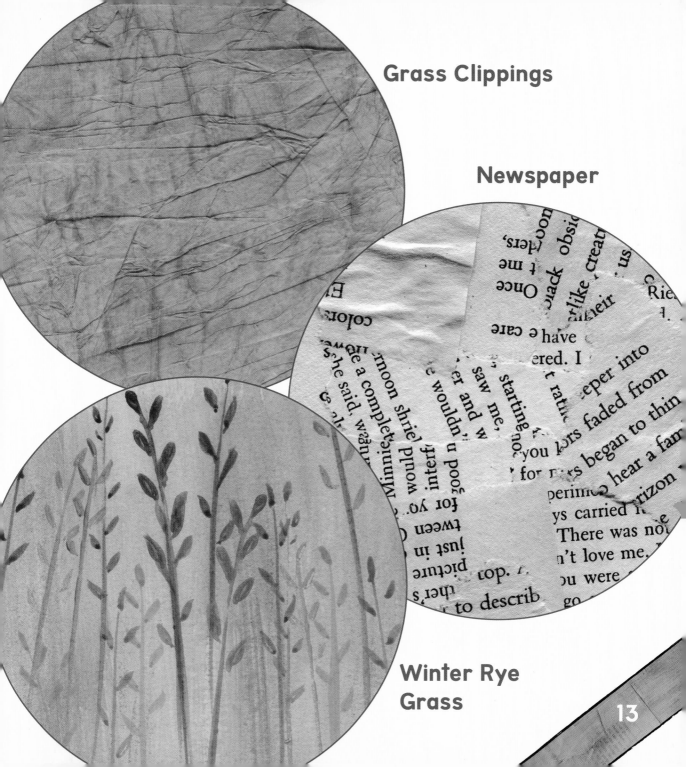

Grass Clippings

Newspaper

Winter Rye Grass

Hungry Plants!

Plants need different foods. But, which foods do they need? A green gardener knows by watching the plants.

One food plants need is nitrogen. It makes their leaves grow. If your plants have yellow or light green leaves, they need nitrogen. This food comes from dead animals.

Many years ago, Native Americans put dead fish in the ground with their corn seeds. This helped the corn grow. Today, you cannot do that. It would smell bad. But, you can use fish emulsion to provide plants nitrogen.

Plants are like vampires. They need blood to get nitrogen. You can use blood meal to feed plants.

Another food plants need is phosphorus. If a plant's leaves are red or purple, it may need this. Also, if plants are not making flowers, you should add phosphorus.

A green gardener can use two natural things to add phosphorus to a garden. One is bone meal. The other is rock phosphate.

Many green gardeners must add phosphorus before they start their first garden. After that, they can put it into their compost.

The last food plants need is potassium. This food is very important. It helps plants use light. It also helps move water and other foods in the plants.

If your plants are bent over after watering them, they may need potassium. Also, if the fruit on your plant is very small, add it.

You can add potassium by using green sand. It comes from places where oceans were many years ago. It feeds the plants slowly.

Be a Green Gardener

A green gardener knows that worms need food. He or she feeds them with compost, mulch, and dead grass. Then the worms feed the plants.

A green gardener also knows that plants need other foods. He or she feeds them organic things. You are on your way to being a green gardener!

Counting Worms

You will need:

A shovel   A bucket or pail
Some newspaper   Garden gloves

Steps to count worms:

1. Dig out some of the dirt from your garden. Cut a square about 12 inches (30 cm) in length on all four sides. Dig down about 6 to 7 inches (15 to 18 cm).
2. Remove the dirt. Place it in your bucket.
3. Spread the dirt on some newspaper. Carefully pick out the worms. Put the worms on a separate sheet of newspaper.
4. When you have finished, count your worms.
5. If you have less than ten worms, then your soil is not healthy.
6. If you have ten or more worms, you have healthy soil.

Glossary

bacteria: tiny, one-celled organisms that can only be seen through a microscope. Some are germs.

blood meal: an organic fertilizer made from animal blood.

bone meal: an organic fertilizer made from ground-up animal bones.

compost: decaying things that were once alive. It is used to make soil healthy.

fish emulsion: an organic fertilizer made from ground-up fish.

mulch: cut grass, straw, or other things that cover the soil in a garden.

nitrogen: an element found in the air and in the earth.

organic: of, using, or grown without chemical fertilizers or insecticides.

Web Sites

To learn more about green gardening, visit ABDO Group online. Web sites about green gardening are featured on our Book Links page. These links are routinely monitored and updated to provide the most current information available.

www.abdopublishing.com

Index